A LITTLE BIT OF

Shakespeare

A LITTLE BIT OF SHAKESPEARE WIT

Copyright © Summersdale Publishers, 2012

Summersdale Publishers Ltd
46 West Street
Chichester
West Sussex
PO19 1RP
UK

www.summersdale.com

Printed and bound in Great Britain

ISBN: 978-1-84953-308-9

Substantial discounts on bulk quantities of Summersdale books are available to corporations, professional associations and other organisations. For details telephone Summersdale Publishers on (+44-1243-771107), fax (+44-1243-786300) or email (nicky@summersdale.com).

A LITTLE BIT OF

Shakespeare
Wit

**EDWARD
GREEN**

summersdale

Contents

He's winding up the
watch of his wit;
By and by it will strike.

Sebastian, *The Tempest*,
Act II, Scene I

Editor's Note

Friends, Romans, countrymen... make yourself comfortable and prepare to be dazzled by the trenchant wordplay of our favourite playwright.

Bloody daggers, scurvy companions and orange Counts; fortune, luck and honesty; fools, friends and lovers – Shakespeare had something witty to say about every situation. In the second act of *King Richard II*, John of Gaunt says, wisely, 'Where words are scarce, they are seldom spent in vain'. This small but perfectly formed volume of Shakespeare's best quips, quotes and comebacks proves his point perfectly, showing once and for all that it is quality, not quantity, which matters.

WISE WORDS
AND ADVICE

Give every man thy ear,
but few thy voice.

Polonius, *Hamlet*, Act I, Scene III

Have more than thou showest,

Speak less than thou knowest,

Lend less than thou owest.

Fool, *King Lear*, Act I, Scene IV

What's in a name?
That which we call a rose
By any other name would
smell as sweet.

Juliet, *Romeo and Juliet*, Act II, Scene II

Be cheque'd for silence,
But never tax'd for speech.

**Countess, *All's Well That Ends Well*,
Act I, Scene I**

Rich gifts wax poor when
givers prove unkind.

Ophelia, *Hamlet*, Act III, Scene I

Why then, can one desire too
much of a good thing?

**Rosalind, *As You Like It*,
Act IV, Scene I**

Wisely, and slow; they
stumble that run fast.

**Friar Laurence, *Romeo and Juliet*,
Act II, Scene III**

There is nothing either good or
bad, but thinking makes it so.

Hamlet, *Hamlet*, Act II, Scene II

All the world's a stage,
And all the men and
women merely players:
They have their exits
and their entrances;
And one man in his time
plays many parts,
His acts being seven ages.

Jaques, *As You Like It*, Act II, Scene VII

The web of our life is of a mingled yarn, good and ill together: our virtues would be proud, if our faults whipped them not; and our crimes would despair, if they were not cherished by our virtues.

First Lord, *All's Well That Ends Well*, Act IV, Scene III

O, swear not by the moon,
th' inconstant moon,
That monthly changes
in her circled orb,
Lest that thy love prove
likewise variable.

**Juliet, *Romeo and Juliet*,
Act II, Scene II**

But, O, how bitter a thing
it is to look into happiness
through another man's eyes!
By so much the more shall I
to-morrow be at the height of
heart-heaviness, by how much
I shall think my brother happy
in having what he wishes for.

**Orlando, *As You Like It*,
Act V, Scene II**

When sorrows come, they
come not single spies
But in battalions.

**King Claudius, *Hamlet*,
Act IV, Scene V**

—◆—

Tempt not a desperate man.

**Romeo, *Romeo and Juliet*,
Act V, Scene III**

—◆—

Well, every one can master
a grief but he that has it.

Benedick, *Much Ado About Nothing*,
Act IV, Scene II

This above all,
– to thine ownself be true;
And it must follow,
as the night the day,
Thou canst not then be
false to any man.

Polonius, *Hamlet*, Act I, Scene III

THE COURSE
OF TRUE LOVE

Ay me! for aught that I could ever read,
Could ever hear by tale or history,
The course of true love
never did run smooth.

**Lysander, *A Midsummer Night's
Dream*, Act I, Scene I**

Bid me discourse, I will
enchant thine ear,
Or like a fairy trip upon the green,
Or, like a nymph, with
long dishevell'd hair,
Dance on the sands, and
yet no footing seen:
Love is a spirit all compact of fire,
Not gross to sink, but
light, and will aspire.

'Venus and Adonis'

If love be blind, love
cannot hit the mark.

**Mercutio, *Romeo and Juliet*,
Act II, Scene I**

I had rather hear my dog
bark at a crow, than a man
swear he loves me.

**Beatrice, *Much Ado About Nothing*,
Act I, Scene I**

Love sought is good, but
given unsought better.

**Olivia, *Twelfth Night*,
Act III, Scene I**

I pray you, do not fall
in love with me,
For I am falser than vows
made in wine.

Rosalind, *As You Like It*, Act III, Scene V

NERISSA: How like you the young German, the Duke of Saxony's nephew?

PORTIA: Very vilely in the morning, when he is sober, and most vilely in the afternoon, when he is drunk: when he is best, he is a little worse than a man, and when he is worst, he is little better than a beast.

The Merchant of Venice, **Act I, Scene II**

———•———

Romeo! humours! madman!
passion! lover!
Appear thou in the
likeness of a sigh.

Mercutio, *Romeo and Juliet*,
Act II, Scene I

———•———

Let every eye negotiate for itself,
And trust no agent;
for beauty is a witch,
Against whose charms faith
melteth into blood.

**Claudio, *Much Ado About Nothing*,
Act II, Scene I**

Let me not to the marriage
of true minds
Admit impediments.
Love is not love
Which alters when it
alteration finds,
Or bends with the
remover to remove: –
O no! it is an ever-fixed mark
That looks on tempests,
and is never shaken.

Sonnet 116

Good night, good night! Parting is
such sweet sorrow,
That I shall say good night
till it be morrow.

Juliet, *Romeo and Juliet*, Act II, Scene II

But love is blind,
and lovers cannot see
The pretty follies that
themselves commit.

**Jessica, *The Merchant of Venice*,
Act II, Scene VI**

Doubt thou the stars are fire;
Doubt that the sun doth move;
Doubt truth to be a liar;
But never doubt I love.

**Polonius (reading a letter
from Hamlet to Ophelia),
Hamlet, Act II, Scene II**

Love looks not with the
eyes, but with the mind.

**Helena, *A Midsummer Night's
Dream*, Act I, Scene I**

See, how she leans her
cheek upon her hand!
O, that I were a glove
upon that hand,
That I might touch that cheek!

**Romeo, *Romeo and Juliet*,
Act II, Scene II**

MUSIC AND NATURE

If music be the food of love, play on;
Give me excess of it,
that, surfeiting,
The appetite may
sicken, and so die.

Orsino, *Twelfth Night*, Act I, Scene I

The man that hath no
music in himself,
Nor is not mov'd with
concord of sweet sounds,
Is fit for treasons,
stratagems, and spoils;
The motions of his spirit
are dull as night,
And his affections dark as Erebus:
Let no such man be trusted.

**Lorenzo, *The Merchant of Venice*,
Act V, Scene I**

The cuckoo then, on every tree,
Mocks married men,
for thus sings he,
Cuckoo;
Cuckoo, cuckoo: O, word of fear,
Unpleasing to a married ear!

**'Spring', *Love's Labour's Lost*,
Act V, Scene II**

I can suck melancholy out of a song, as a weasel sucks eggs.

Jaques, *As You Like It*, Act II, Scene V

Be not afeard;
the isle is full of noises,
Sounds, and sweet airs, that
give delight and hurt not.

Caliban, *The Tempest*, Act III, Scene II

———•———

This shadowy desert,
unfrequented woods,
I better brook than flourishing
peopled towns.

**Valentine, *The Two Gentlemen
of Verona*, Act V, Scene IV**

———•———

O, wonder!
How many goodly creatures
are there here!
How beauteous mankind
is! O brave new world,
That has such people in't!

Miranda, *The Tempest*, Act V, Scene I

One touch of nature makes
the whole world kin.

**Ulysses, *Troilus and Cressida*,
Act III, Scene III**

The sun's a thief, and with
his great attraction
Robs the vast sea; the
moon's an arrant thief,
And her pale fire she
snatches from the sun.

**Timon, *Timon of Athens*,
Act IV, Scene III**

LUCK AND FORTUNE

When beggars die,
there are no comets seen;
The heavens themselves blaze
forth the death of princes.

**Calpurnia, *Julius Caesar*,
Act II, Scene II**

———◆———

Why, then the world's mine oyster,
Which I with sword will open.

**Pistol, *The Merry Wives of Windsor*,
Act II, Scene II**

———◆———

The world is grown so bad,
That wrens make prey where
eagles dare not perch:
Since every Jack
became a gentleman
There's many a gentle
person made a Jack.

**Gloucester, *King Richard III*,
Act I, Scene III**

Luck and Fortune

Let us sit and mock the good
housewife Fortune from her wheel,
that her gifts may henceforth
be bestowed equally…
For those that she makes fair
she scarce makes honest, and
those that she makes honest
she makes very ill-favouredly.

Celia, *As You Like It*, Act I, Scene II

Truly, shepherd, in respect of itself,
it is a good life; but in respect that
it is a shepherd's life, it is naught.
In respect that it is solitary, I like
it very well; but in respect that
it is private, it is a very vile life.
Now in respect it is in the fields,
it pleaseth me well; but in respect
it is not in the court, it is tedious.

**Touchstone, *As You Like It*,
Act III, Scene II**

And worse I may be yet:
the worst is not
So long as we can say
'This is the worst.'

Edgar, *King Lear*, Act IV, Scene I

—◆—

Henry now lives in Scotland,
at his ease;
Where having nothing,
nothing he can lose.

**Warwick, *Henry VI, Part III*,
Act III, Scene III**

—◆—

Ne'er ask me what raiment I'll wear; for I have no more doublets than backs, no more stockings than legs, nor no more shoes than feet; nay, sometimes more feet than shoes, or such shoes as my toes look through the over-leather.

**Sly, *The Taming of the Shrew*,
Induction, Scene II**

The robb'd that smiles steals
something from the thief.

**Duke of Venice, *Othello*,
Act I, Scene III**

But be not afraid of greatness:
some are born great, some
achieve greatness, and some have
greatness thrust upon 'em.

**Malvolio, *Twelfth Night,*
Act II, Scene V**

.

❧

True is it that we have
seen better days.

**Duke Senior, *As You Like It*,
Act II, Scene VII**

❧

Why, man, he doth bestride
the narrow world
Like a Colossus, and we petty men
Walk under his huge legs
and peep about
To find ourselves
dishonourable graves.

Cassius, *Julius Caesar*, Act I, Scene II

By the pricking of my thumbs,
Something wicked this way comes.
Open, locks,
Whoever knocks!

**Second Witch, *Macbeth*,
Act IV, Scene I**

Luck and Fortune

[Singing]
He that has and a little tiny wit –
With hey, ho,
the wind and the rain, –
Must make content with
his fortunes fit,
For the rain it raineth every day.

Fool, *King Lear*, Act III, Scene II

Am not I Christopher Sly, old Sly's son of Burton Heath; by birth a pedlar, by education a cardmaker, by transmutation a bear-herd, and now by present profession a tinker?

Sly, *The Taming of the Shrew*, Induction, Scene II

FRIENDS AND ENEMIES

Friendship is constant
in all other things,
Save in the office and affairs of love.

**Claudio, *Much Ado About Nothing*,
Act II, Scene I**

Neither a borrower nor a lender be;
For loan oft loses both
itself and friend,
And borrowing dulls the
edge of husbandry.

Polonius, *Hamlet*, Act I, Scene III

Heat not a furnace for your foe
so hot that it do singe yourself.

**Duke of Norfolk, *Henry VIII*,
Act I, Scene I**

JAQUES: God be wi' you: let's meet as little as we can.

ORLANDO: I do desire we may be better strangers.

As You Like It, Act III, Scene II

Love all, trust a few,
Do wrong to none: be
able for thine enemy
Rather in power than use,
and keep thy friend
Under thy own life's key.

**Countess, *All's Well That Ends Well*,
Act I, Scene I**

If thou wilt lend this money...
lend it rather to thine enemy;
Who, if he break, thou
may'st with better face
Exact the penalty.

**Antonio, *The Merchant of Venice*,
Act I, Scene III**

Friends and Enemies

I wonder men dare trust
themselves with men...
The fellow that
Sits next him now, parts bread
with him, and pledges
The breath of him in a
divided draught,
Is the readiest man to kill
him: it has been proved.

**Apemantus, *Timon of Athens*,
Act I, Scene II**

'Sblood, do you think I am easier
to be played on than a pipe?
Call me what instrument you
will, though you can fret me,
yet you cannot play upon me.

Hamlet, *Hamlet*, Act III, Scene II

Friends and Enemies

Let me have men about
me that are fat;
Sleek-headed men and such
as sleep o' nights:
Yond Cassius has a lean
and hungry look;
He thinks too much:
such men are dangerous.

**Julius Caesar, *Julius Caesar*,
Act I, Scene II**

Nature teaches beasts to
know their friends.

Sicinius, *Coriolanus*, Act II, Scene I

If you prick us, do we not bleed?
if you tickle us, do we not laugh?
if you poison us, do we not die?
and if you wrong us, shall
we not revenge?

**Shylock, *The Merchant of Venice*,
Act III, Scene I**

JAQUES: Rosalind is
your love's name?
ORLANDO: Yes, just.
JAQUES: I do not like her name.
ORLANDO: There was no
thought of pleasing you
when she was christened.

As You Like It, **Act III, Scene II**

FOOLS, MADMEN AND DRUNKARDS

Better a witty fool than
a foolish wit.

Clown, *Twelfth Night*, Act I, Scene V

Lord what fools these mortals be!

Puck, *A Midsummer Night's Dream*, Act III, Scene II

He's mad that trusts in
the tameness of a wolf,
a horse's health, a boy's
love, or a whore's oath.

Fool, *King Lear*, Act III, Scene VI

He was, for all the world,
like a forked radish, with a
head fantastically carved
upon it with a knife.

**Falstaff, *Henry IV, Part II*,
Act III, Scene II**

———◆———

CASSIO: Is your Englishman so expert in his drinking?
IAGO: Why, he drinks you, with facility, your Dane dead drunk; he sweats not to overthrow your Almain; he gives your Hollander a vomit, ere the next pottle can be filled.

***Othello*, Act II, Scene III**

———◆———

MACDUFF: What three things does drink especially provoke?
PORTER: Marry, sir, nose-painting, sleep, and urine. Lechery, sir, it provokes, and unprovokes: it provokes the desire, but it takes away the performance.

Macbeth, **Act II, Scene III**

There shall be in England seven
half-penny loaves sold for a
penny; the three-hooped
pot shall have ten hoops; and I will
make it felony to drink small beer.

**Cade, *Henry VI, Part II*,
Act IV, Scene II**

These clothes are good enough to drink in; and so be these boots too: and they be not, let them hang themselves in their own straps.

Sir Toby Belch, *Twelfth Night*, Act I, Scene III

Leave thy drink and thy whore,
And keep in-a-door,
And thou shalt have more
Than two tens to a score.

Fool, *King Lear*, Act I, Scene IV

Though this be madness,
yet there is method in 't.

Polonius, *Hamlet*, Act II, Scene II

Why, thou say'st well.
I do now remember a saying:
'The fool doth think he is wise,
but the wise man
knows himself to be a fool.'

**Touchstone, *As You Like It*,
Act V, Scene I**

OLIVIA: What's a drunken man like, fool?

CLOWN: Like a drown'd man, a fool and a mad man: one draught above heat makes him a fool; the second mads him; and a third drowns him.

Twelfth Night, **Act I, Scene V**

I'll drink no more than will do me good, for no man's pleasure, I.

Mistress Quickly, *Henry IV, Part II*, Act II, Scene IV

SIR TOBY BELCH: Does not our
life consist of the four elements?
SIR ANDREW AGUE-CHEEK:
Faith, so they say; but I
think it rather consists
of eating and drinking.

Twelfth Night, **Act II, Scene III**

Ask Marian Hacket, the fat
ale-wife of Wincot, if she know
me not: if she say I am not
fourteen pence on the score for
sheer ale, score me up for the
lyingest knave in Christendom.

**Sly, *The Taming of the Shrew*,
Induction, Scene II**

VIRTUES AND VICES

Well, heaven forgive him!
and forgive us all!
Some rise by sin, and
some by virtue fall.

**Escalus, *Measure for Measure*,
Act II, Scene I**

The better part of valour is
discretion; in the which better
part I have saved my life.

**Falstaff, *Henry IV, Part I*,
Act V, Scene IV**

Ha, ha! What a fool Honesty
is! and Trust, his sworn brother,
a very simple gentleman!

**Autolycus, *The Winter's Tale*,
Act IV, Scene IV**

How poor are they that
have not patience!
What wound did ever
heal but by degrees?

Iago, *Othello*, Act II, Scene III

Lord, Lord, how subject we old men are to this vice of lying! This same starved justice hath done nothing but prate to me of the wildness of his youth, and the feats he hath done about Turnbull Street: and every third word a lie.

Falstaff, *Henry IV, Part II*, Act III, Scene II

I am in blood
Stepp'd in so far that,
should I wade no more,
Returning were as tedious as go o'er:
Strange things I have in head,
that will to hand,
Which must be acted ere
they may be scann'd.

Macbeth, *Macbeth*, Act III, Scene IV

Let not our babbling dreams
affright our souls;
Conscience is but a word
that cowards use.

**King Richard III, *King Richard III*,
Act V, Scene III**

The devil can cite Scripture
for his purpose.
An evil soul, producing holy witness,
Is like a villain with a smiling cheek,
A goodly apple rotten at the heart.

**Antonio, *The Merchant of Venice*,
Act I, Scene III**

Our doubts are traitors,
And make us lose the good
we oft might win
By fearing to attempt.

**Lucio, *Measure for Measure*,
Act I, Scene IV**

Suspicion always haunts
the guilty mind;
The thief doth fear each
bush an officer.

**Gloucester, *Henry VI, Part III*,
Act V, Scene VI**

March on, join bravely,
let us to't pell-mell;
If not to heaven, then
hand in hand to hell.

**King Richard III, *King Richard III*,
Act V, Scene III**

For there was never yet philosopher
That could endure the
toothache patiently,
However they have writ
the style of gods
And made a push at
chance and sufferance.

**Leonato, *Much Ado About Nothing*,
Act V, Scene I**

———•———

Of all base passions fear
is most accursed.

**Joan La Pucelle, *Henry VI, Part I*,
Act V, Scene II**

———•———

I dare do all that may become a man;

Who dares do more is none.

Macbeth, *Macbeth*, Act I, Scene VII

Who 'scapes the lurking
serpent's mortal sting?
Not he that sets his
foot upon her back.
The smallest worm will
turn being trodden on;
And doves will peck in
safeguard of their brood.

**Clifford, *Henry VI, Part III*,
Act II, Scene II**

When that the poor have
cried, Caesar hath wept;
Ambition should be made
of sterner stuff:
Yet Brutus says he was ambitious;
And Brutus is an honourable man.

Antony, *Julius Caesar*, Act III, Scene II

There's no more valour in that
Poins than in a wild duck.

Falstaff, *Henry IV, Part I*, Act II, Scene II

True nobility is exempt from fear.

Suffolk, *Henry VI, Part II*,

Act IV, Scene I

Your face, my Thane, is as
a book where men
May read strange matters.
To beguile the time,
Look like the time; bear
welcome in your eye,
Your hand, your tongue; look like
the innocent flower,
But be the serpent under it.

Lady Macbeth, *Macbeth*, Act I, Scene V

WICKED INSULTS

Asses are made to bear,
and so are you.

**Katherina, *The Taming of the Shrew*,
Act II, Scene I**

O Lord, he will hang upon him like a disease: he is sooner caught than the pestilence, and the taker runs presently mad. God help the noble Claudio! If he have caught the Benedick, it will cost him a thousand pound ere a' be cured.

Beatrice, *Much Ado About Nothing*, Act I, Scene I

O thou caitiff! O thou varlet!
O thou wicked Hannibal!

**Elbow, *Measure for Measure*,
Act II, Scene I**

Why, thou unconfinable baseness!

**Falstaff, *The Merry Wives
of Windsor*, Act II, Scene II**

I scorn you, scurvy companion.
What, you poor, base,
rascally, cheating,
lack-linen mate!
Away, you mouldy rogue, away!

**Doll Tearsheet, *Henry IV, Part II*,
Act II, Scene IV**

Drones suck not eagles'
blood but rob beehives:
It is impossible that I should die
By such a lowly vassal as thyself.

**Suffolk, *Henry VI, Part II*,
Act IV, Scene I**

I would thou didst itch from head
to foot and I had the scratching
of thee; I would make thee the
loathsomest scab in Greece.

**Thersites, *Troilus and Cressida*,
Act II, Scene I**

Unless hours were cups of sack, and minutes capons, and clocks the tongues of bawds, and dials the signs of leaping-houses, and the blessed sun himself a fair hot wench in flame-coloured taffeta; I see no reason why thou should'st be so superfluous, to demand the time of the day.

Prince Henry, *Henry IV, Part I*, Act I, Scene II

BENEDICK: What, my dear Lady Disdain! Are you yet living? BEATRICE: Is it possible Disdain should die, while she hath such meet food to feed it as Signior Benedick? Courtesy itself must convert to disdain, if you come in her presence.

Much Ado About Nothing,
Act I, Scene I

Has Page any brains? hath he any eyes? hath he any thinking? Sure, they sleep; he hath no use of them.

Ford, *The Merry Wives of Windsor*, Act III, Scene II

Would thou wert clean
enough to spit upon!

**Timon, *Timon of Athens*,
Act IV, Scene III**

Thou sodden-witted lord!
thou hast no more brain than
I have in mine elbows.

**Thersites, *Troilus and Cressida*,
Act II, Scene I**

Sir, if you spend word for
word with me, I shall make
your wit bankrupt.

**Thurio, *The Two Gentlemen of
Verona*, Act II, Scene IV**

ESCALUS: What's your
name, Master Tapster?
POMPEY: Pompey.
ESCALUS: What else?
POMPEY: Bum, sir.
ESCALUS: Troth, and your bum
is the greatest thing about you;
so that in the beastliest sense
you are Pompey the Great.

Measure for Measure, **Act II, Scene I**

O that I were a god,
to shoot forth thunder
Upon these paltry, servile,
abject drudges!

**Suffolk, *Henry VI, Part II*,
Act IV, Scene I**

When you speak best unto the purpose, it is not worth the wagging of your beards; and your beards deserve not so honourable a grave as to stuff a botcher's cushion, or to be entombed in an ass's pack-saddle… God-den to your worships: more of your conversation would infect my brain.

Menenius, *Coriolanus*, Act II, Scene I

He is deformed, crooked, old and sere,
Ill-faced, worse bodied,
shapeless everywhere;
Vicious, ungentle, foolish,
blunt, unkind;
Stigmatical in making,
worse in mind.

**Adriana, *The Comedy of Errors*,
Act IV, Scene II**

Go prick thy face,
and over-red thy fear,
Thou lily-liver'd boy.

Macbeth, *Macbeth*, Act V, Scene III

Why, thou clay-brained guts, thou knotty-pated fool, thou whoreson, obscene greasy tallow-catch!

Prince Henry, *Henry IV, Part I*, Act II, Scene IV

Come, you are a tedious
fool: to the purpose.

**Escalus, *Measure for Measure*,
Act II, Scene I**

THIS MORTAL COIL

So wise so young, they
say, do never live long.

**Gloucester, *King Richard III*,
Act III, Scene I**

To be, or not to be: that
is the question:
Whether 'tis nobler in
the mind to suffer
The slings and arrows of
outrageous fortune,
Or to take arms against
a sea of troubles,
And by opposing end them?

Hamlet, *Hamlet*, Act III, Scene I

To die: to sleep;
No more; and by a sleep
to say we end
The heart-ache and the
thousand natural shocks
That flesh is heir to, 'tis
a consummation
Devoutly to be wish'd.

Hamlet, *Hamlet*, Act III, Scene I

Out, out, brief candle!
Life's but a walking
shadow, a poor player
That struts and frets his
hour upon the stage
And then is heard no
more: it is a tale
Told by an idiot, full of
sound and fury,
Signifying nothing.

Macbeth, *Macbeth*, Act V, Scene V

Cowards die many times
before their deaths;
The valiant never taste
of death but once.

**Julius Caesar, *Julius Caesar*,
Act II, Scene II**

If thou art rich, thou'rt poor;
For, like an ass whose back
with ingots bows,
Thou bear'st thy heavy
riches but a journey,
And Death unloads thee.

Duke Vincentio, *Measure for Measure*, Act III, Scene I

The comfort is you shall be called
to no more payments, fear no
more tavern bills.

**First Gaoler, *Cymbeline*,
Act V, Scene IV**

Like as the waves make
towards the pebbled shore,
So do our minutes
hasten to their end.

Sonnet 60

Friends, Romans, countrymen,
lend me your ears!
I come to bury Caesar,
not to praise him.
The evil that men do
lives after them;
The good is oft interred
with their bones;
So let it be with Caesar.

Antony, *Julius Caesar*, Act III, Scene II

Nothing in his life
Became him like the
leaving it; he died
As one that had been
studied in his death,
To throw away the dearest
thing he owed,
As 'twere a careless trifle.

Malcolm, *Macbeth*, Act I, Scene IV

We are such stuff
As dreams are made on;
and our little life
Is rounded with a sleep.

Prospero, *The Tempest*, Act IV, Scene I

Thou'rt by no means valiant;
For thou dost fear the
soft and tender fork
Of a poor worm.

Duke Vincentio, *Measure for Measure*, Act III, Scene I

Bear with me;
My heart is in the coffin
there with Caesar,
And I must pause till it
come back to me.

Antony, *Julius Caesar*, Act III, Scene II

The raven himself is hoarse
That croaks the fatal
entrance of Duncan
Under my battlements.

Lady Macbeth, *Macbeth*, Act I, Scene V

WORDS, WORDS, WORDS

POLONIUS: What do
you read, my lord?
HAMLET: Words, words, words.

***Hamlet*, Act II, Scene II**

Where words are scarce, they
are seldom spent in vain;
For they breathe truth that
breathe their words in pain.

**John of Gaunt, *King Richard II*,
Act II, Scene I**

Unhappy that I am, I cannot heave
My heart into my mouth.

Cordelia, *King Lear*, Act I, Scene I

Rude am I in my speech,
And little bless'd with the
soft phrase of peace.

Othello, *Othello*, Act I, Scene III

These words are razors to
my wounded heart.

**Titus Andronicus, *Titus Andronicus*,
Act I, Scene I**

Those that understood him smiled at one another and shook their heads; but, for mine own part, it was Greek to me.

Casca, *Julius Caesar*, Act I, Scene II

Pay her the debt you owe her, and unpay the villainy you have done her: the one you may do with sterling money, and the other with current repentance.

Lord Chief Justice, *Henry IV, Part II*, Act II, Scene I

My liege, and madam, to expostulate
What majesty should be,
what duty is,
Why day is day, night night,
and time is time,
Were nothing but to
waste night, day and time.
Therefore, since brevity
is the soul of wit,
And tediousness the limbs
and outward flourishes,
I will be brief.

Polonius, *Hamlet*, Act II, Scene II

For Nym, he hath heard that
men of few words are the
best men; and therefore he
scorns to say his prayers, lest a'
should be thought a coward.

Boy, *Henry V*, Act III, Scene II

They have been at a great feast of languages, and stolen the scraps.

Moth, *Love's Labour's Lost*, Act V, Scene I

Words more sweet, and
yet more dangerous,
Than baits to fish.

**Tamora, *Titus Andronicus*,
Act IV, Scene IV**

—•—

Weigh'st thy words before
thou giv'st them breath.

Othello, *Othello*, Act III, Scene III

—•—

Let me be cruel, not unnatural:
I will speak daggers to her,
but use none;
My tongue and soul in
this be hypocrites.

Hamlet, *Hamlet*, Act III, Scene II

JAQUES: I pray you, mar no more trees with writing love-songs in their barks.
ORLANDO: I pray you, mar no more of my verses with reading them ill-favouredly.

As You Like It, Act III, Scene II

The count is neither sad, nor sick, nor merry, nor well; but civil count – civil as an orange, and something of that jealous complexion.

Beatrice, *Much Ado About Nothing*, Act II, Scene I

Not marble, nor the
gilded monuments
Of princes, shall outlive
this powerful rhyme.

Sonnet 55

If you're interested in finding out more about our humour books, follow us on Twitter:

@SummersdaleLOL

www.summersdale.com